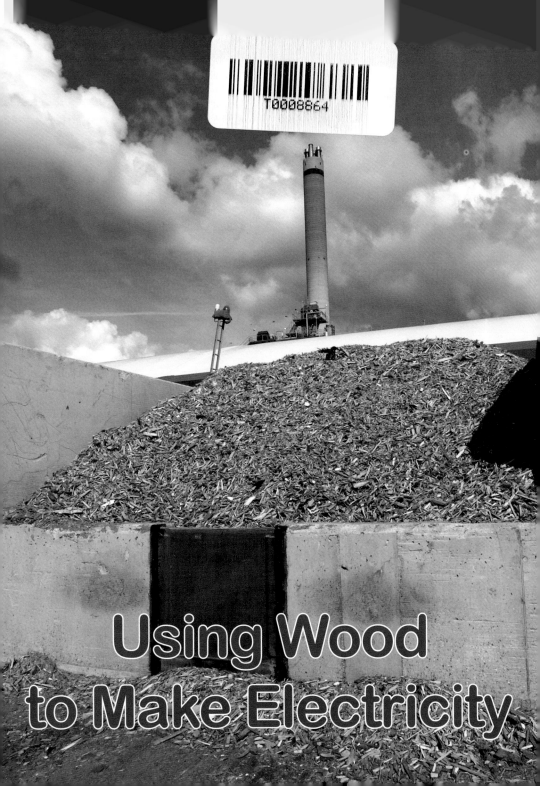

Using Wood to Make Electricity

We can make electricity.

The sun can make electricity.

The wind can make electricity.

The water can make electricity.

Look at this.

This is wood. The wood can make electricity too.

The wood goes in the fire.

The fire will make

the water hot.

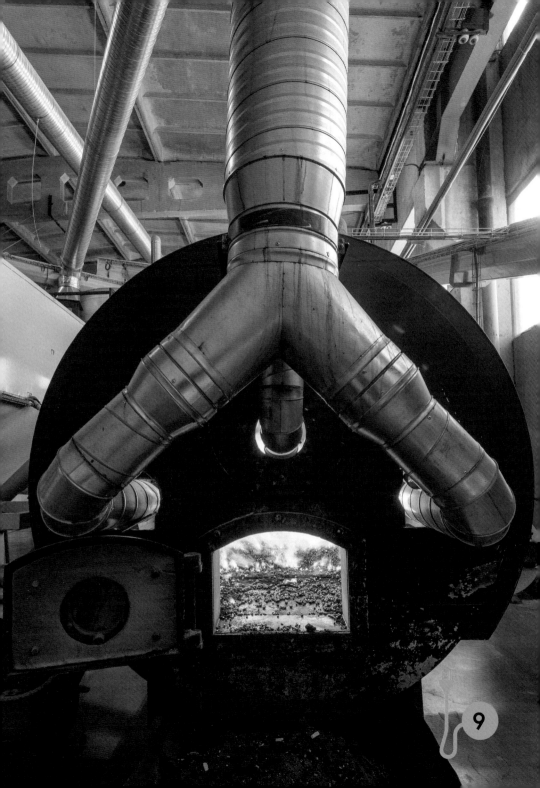

Bubble. Bubble. Bubble.

The water is hot.

Can you see the **steam**?

The steam is hot.

The steam will go
on the **wheel**.
The steam will make
the wheel go round
and round.
This will make electricity.

The electricity is made here.

Glossary

 steam

 wheel

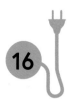